MONARCH BUTTERFLIES
— A GENERATIONAL JOURNEY —

REBECCA HIRSCH
AND MARIA KORAN

www.av2books.com

MEDIA ENHANCED BOOKS
AV²
BY WEIGL™
ADDED VALUE • AUDIO VISUAL

AV² provides enriched content that supplements and complements this book. Weigl's AV² books strive to create inspired learning and engage young minds in a total learning experience.

Your AV² Media Enhanced books come alive with...

Audio
Listen to sections of the book read aloud.

Key Words
Study vocabulary, and complete a matching word activity.

Go to **www.av2books.com**, and enter this book's unique code.

Video
Watch informative video clips.

Quizzes
Test your knowledge.

BOOK CODE

Y 5 3 5 5 7 2

Embedded Weblinks
Gain additional information for research.

Slide Show
View images and captions, and prepare a presentation.

AV² by Weigl brings you media enhanced books that support active learning.

Try This!
Complete activities and hands-on experiments.

... and much, much more!

Published by AV² by Weigl
350 5th Avenue, 59th Floor
New York, NY 10118
Website: www.av2books.com

Library of Congress Cataloging-in-Publication Data

Names: Hirsch, Rebecca E., and Koran, Maria.
Title: Monarch butterflies : a generational journey / Rebecca Hirsch and Maria Koran.
Description: New York, NY : AV2 by Weigl, [2017] | Series: Nature's great
  journeys | Includes bibliographical references and index.
Identifiers: LCCN 2016004430| ISBN 9781489645210 (hard cover : alk. paper) |
  ISBN 9781489649942 (soft cover : alk. paper) | ISBN 9781489645227 (Multi-user ebk.)
Subjects: LCSH: Monarch butterfly--Migration--Juvenile literature. | Monarch
  butterfly--Juvenile literature. | Animal migration--Juvenile literature.
Classification: LCC QL561.D3 H57 2017 | DDC 595.78/9--dc23
LC record available at http://lccn.loc.gov/2016004430

Printed in the United States of America in Brainerd, Minnesota
1 2 3 4 5 6 7 8 9 0 20 19 18 17 16

072016
071416

Project Coordinator: Maria Koran   Art Director: Terry Paulhus

Every reasonable effort has been made to trace ownership and to obtain permission to reprint copyright material. The publishers would be pleased to have any errors or omissions brought to their attention so that they may be corrected in subsequent printings.

Weigl acknowledges Getty Images, Dreamstime, Alamy, Minden, and Shutterstock as its primary image suppliers for this title.

Contents

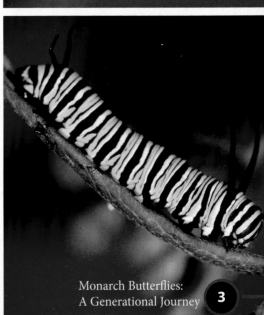

MONARCH BUTTERFLIES

Every fall something wonderful happens across North America. Millions of monarch butterflies from across North America fly south. They travel up to 3,000 miles (4,800 km). They fly all the way to Mexico, Florida, and Southern California. The monarch's black and orange wings look delicate. They are very strong, though. Monarch butterflies complete the longest journey of any insect on Earth.

The monarchs' lifetime journey is their migration. This is when an animal moves from one **habitat** to another. Migrations happen for many reasons. Some animals move to be in warmer weather where there is more food. There they can reproduce, or have their babies. And these migrations can be short distances, such as from a mountaintop to its valley. Or they can be long distances, like the monarch's flight.

A monarch butterfly has strong wings.

MIGRATION MAP

Monarch butterflies fly by several paths on their **seasonal** migration. Monarchs by the Great Lakes fly straight toward Texas and Mexico. Monarchs in New England fly along the coast of the Atlantic Ocean. Monarchs in the West follow the coast of the Pacific Ocean

The monarchs from the middle and eastern parts of North America end up in central Mexico and Florida. The monarchs from western North America travel to southern California. Some go to western parts of Mexico for the winter.

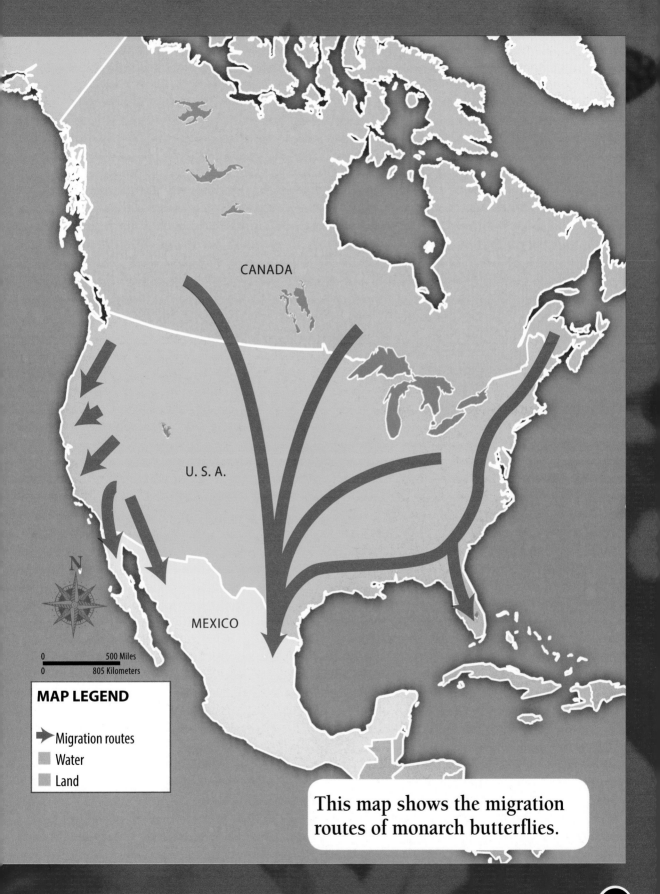

CANADA

U. S. A.

N

MEXICO

0   500 Miles
0   805 Kilometers

MAP LEGEND

➤ Migration routes
◼ Water
◼ Land

This map shows the migration routes of monarch butterflies.

Each female monarch only lays
only one egg on a milkweed plant.

BECOMING A BUTTERFLY

Monarchs live in fields, meadows, and gardens. Life begins on a milkweed plant. It is the monarch butterfly's **host plant**. A female butterfly finds a milkweed plant. She is ready to lay her eggs. She chooses a leaf near the top of the plant. She glues one egg to the underside of the leaf.

After a few days the egg **hatches**. A caterpillar crawls out. The caterpillar eats and grows. First it eats its eggshell. Then it eats the milkweed plant. The caterpillar needs to grow and store energy. It needs energy for its **metamorphosis**. This is its change from a caterpillar to a butterfly. The caterpillar **molts** as it grows. It spins some silk. It sticks the silk to a leaf. Then it wiggles out of its old skin. Fresh new skin is underneath.

The caterpillar is the larval stage of the butterfly life cycle. This stage lasts up to 14 days.

Monarch caterpillars
change into butterflies.

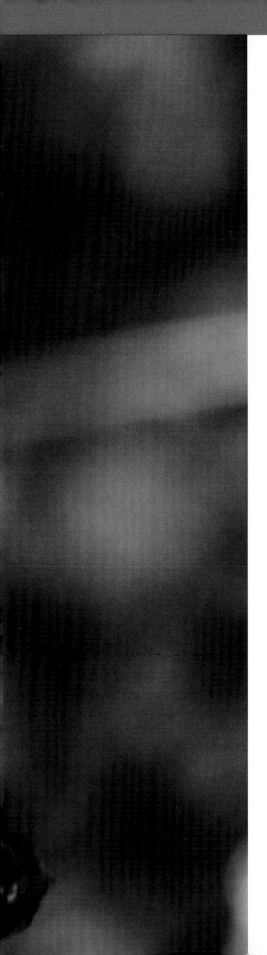

Monarch caterpillars have colors on their bodies. The colors warn **predators**. The caterpillars eat only milkweed. They absorb milkweed poisons into their bodies. The poisons do not harm the caterpillars. The poisons can make birds and other animals sick, though. Predators stay away from the brightly striped caterpillars.

The caterpillar is ready for a big change in its body. It hangs upside down and sheds its skin one last time. It is now a **pupa**. The pupa's skin becomes a pale green **chrysalis**. Two weeks pass. The pupa's body changes inside the chrysalis. Then the chrysalis splits open. An adult butterfly crawls out. It hangs upside down to dry its wings. Then it flies off to look for food.

Male and female monarchs have slightly different markings on their wings.

LIFE IN THE SUMMER

An adult butterfly is not a picky eater. It drinks **nectar** from many kinds of flowers. It spots the flowers with its eyes. It finds the nectar on the flower using its feet. Its feet and **antennae** have parts that sense taste. The butterfly uncurls its long **proboscis**. It sucks the sweet nectar from the flower. It **basks** in the sunshine and flaps its wings. This is how it warms its body.

Adult butterflies need to mate to make new butterflies. A male and a female come together to mate. Soon eggs grow in the female's body. Then she searches for milkweed plants to lay her eggs.

Monarch butterflies spend their summers in the meadows. But in late summer, life in the meadow changes. The days get shorter. Cool breezes blow. Winter is on its way. Monarchs cannot survive the freezing northern winters. They must leave their summer habitat. They fly south to survive the winter.

Adult butterflies get their food from flowers.

Female butterflies can taste a plant by standing on it. They taste with all six legs.

FLYING SOUTH

New butterflies grow in late summer. They look the same as other monarchs, but they are different. They do not mate or lay eggs right away. But they do eat a lot of nectar. They store the food as fat in their bodies.

Then these butterflies fly in one direction. They head for Mexico, Florida, or southern California. The butterflies travel about 40 to 100 miles (64 to 160 km) a day. More butterflies join the migration each week. Great clouds of butterflies can be seen in the sky.

Monarchs do not fly in flocks like birds. Each butterfly flies alone. Migrating monarchs soar very high in the sky. They ride air currents. These currents give them a push as they head south.

The monarchs gather in trees at night. They sit in big groups on the branches. This is called roosting. Thousands of monarch butterflies may roost in one tree. They bask in the morning sunlight. Their muscles warm up for another day of flight.

Even though they migrate at the same time, each monarch flies alone.

FINDING THEIR WAY

No one knows how monarchs find their way. Scientists think monarchs use the sun to point the way. The sun moves across the sky. It rises in the east and sets in the west. The butterflies do not follow the sun from east to west, but they may use the sun to find their way. They can tell the time by using their antennae. The antennae can sense where the sun is in the sky. To fly south, the butterflies keep the sun on their left in the morning. In the late afternoon, they keep the sun on their right. Monarchs may also sense the magnetic field inside Earth. This field is what makes a compass point north. The butterflies may have a sort of compass in their bodies.

Butterflies live in different places. But many fly to the same place. They fly in different directions. A monarch in North Dakota flies straight to the south. But one in Indiana flies in a curve to get south. Somehow they all fly in the right direction. These monarch butterflies have never been to their winter homes before.

The monarchs stop for food along their journey.

The sun may be used by monarchs
to help guide them south.

Up to 15,000 monarchs can cluster on one fir branch.

MONARCH WINTERS

In their winter homes, monarchs gather on trees.

In Mexico, all the monarchs go to a few steep mountain ranges. They find the mountain forests. These forests are filled with a type of fir tree. It is called oyamel. The monarchs gather in the trees. There are thousands of monarchs. The butterflies hang from the trunks, branches, and needles. The oyamel branches bend with the weight of the butterflies. Sometimes the branches even break. It sends the butterflies crashing to the ground.

The western monarchs spend their winters in Southern California. The coastal forests there have weather like the Mexican forests.

The mountain forests seem like a strange place for monarchs to spend the winter. There is less food for them to eat. The air in the forest is chilly. It is between 32 and 60 °F (0 and 15 °C). Sometimes it even drops below freezing. Why would butterflies travel to a place that is cold? Why would they travel to a place without enough food?

But the mountain forests are perfect for the monarchs. The forests keep the monarchs safe. The oyamel trees grow close together. Their branches touch. This keeps out deadly winter storms. Fog and clouds settle over the forest. They bring moist air. It keeps the butterflies from drying out.

It is too cold for the butterflies to fly. So, they hang in the trees. Even the lack of food is not a problem. The monarchs do not need to eat. They can live off their stored fat. The cooler temperatures help also. The butterflies use less energy when it is cool.

The butterflies warm up enough to fly on sunny days. They go to a stream for a drink. Or they drop to the ground to sip dew from plants. The butterflies return to the trees as soon as a cloud passes over. Being away from the trees is unsafe. There is danger on the ground. Predators may catch the butterflies. Or the butterflies can get wet and freeze to death.

Resting in forest trees during winter keeps monarchs safe from cold.

FLYING BACK NORTH

The days grow longer and warmer as winter passes. Soon the monarchs become active again. They leave the forests in the second week of March. They go back the way they came. It is time to make the journey north.

But these butterflies will not travel far. They have already completed a 1,000 to 3,000 mile (1,600 to 4,800 km) trip. Their wings are torn. They have little fat left in their bodies. They have lived 8 or 9 months. That is a long life for a butterfly. But now their lives are coming to an end. There is one last thing they must do. They must mate. Then the females find milkweed plants to lay their eggs. After that, the adult butterflies die.

It takes several generations of monarchs for the butterflies to reach their summer homes.

But the migration is not over. The return trip is like a relay. Their children will fly next in the migration. The caterpillars hatch and begin to grow. Soon they become adult butterflies. They continue flying north. These butterflies do not live as long as their parents. They live about a month. But as they fly north they mate. And the females lay eggs. Then they die. Their children will continue the trip.

Two or three more groups of monarchs are born. The last group reaches the monarch's summer homes. The butterflies arrive just as the milkweed has started to grow in the north. Millions and millions of monarchs arrive in the summer. They fly in fields, meadows, and gardens again.

Unlike some butterflies and moths, monarchs do not spin silk cocoons.

In spring, butterflies return to meadows in the north.

Sycamore and other trees monarchs use for homes are being cut down.

HABITAT THREATS

The monarch's migration has changed in the last 100 years. People have caused these changes.

People have destroyed the monarch's summer habitats. They have built roads, houses, and farms in the fields and meadows. Many people think milkweed plants are weeds. They mow milkweed and wildflowers that grow along roads. They spray the plants with a liquid that kills the plants. Without milkweed, monarch caterpillars cannot grow. Without flowers, monarch butterflies cannot eat.

The California forests where monarchs spend the winter have changed. Today monarchs roost in eucalyptus, pine, and cypress trees. Long ago they also roosted in sycamore trees. The sycamores have almost disappeared. They have been cut down. Many worry that the western monarchs' winter home will be destroyed.

There are more problems in the oyamel forests. The eastern monarchs gather in only about 12 places. There can be 100 million monarchs each winter. Any changes can affect the monarchs in a big way. The streams in the forest go dry because people use too much water. Monarchs have to fly farther to find water to drink. Sometimes they cannot make it back to the trees before the cold weather returns.

TAG@KU.EDU
MONARCH WATCH
1-888-TAGGING
GJE 148

Scientists found the Mexican winter
sites of the monarch in 1975. Until
then, only local villagers knew
about the butterflies' winter homes.

The oyamel forests are in danger of being destroyed. The oyamel trees are being cut down. This opens gaps in the forest. The gaps let in snow and rain. This can be deadly for the insects.

All of these changes make the Mexican forests unsafe for monarchs. More butterflies are dying than before.

People from Mexico, the United States, and Canada must work together to solve the monarchs' problems. Scientists study the monarchs. They try to learn how many monarchs are alive each year. They try to understand what harms the butterflies. And they try to find answers. Scientists tell the world about the need to save the monarch butterfly.

In Mexico, people must take care of the forests. They must stop others from cutting down the oyamel trees. In the United States and Canada, people must work to save monarch's habitats.

Many people have already planted butterfly gardens. These gardens are filled with milkweed and nectar plants. They provide food for caterpillars and adult butterflies. They have flowers that bloom during the spring and fall migrations. These gardens act like stepping stones across a stream for the monarchs. They give monarchs places to stop, eat, and continue their journey. These patches of habitat help monarchs survive and continue their glorious migration.

QUIZ

1 Where do monarch butterflies go on their southern migration?

A. To Mexico, Florida, and California

2 What is the newly hatched caterpillar's first meal?

A. Its eggshell

3 What do adult butterflies eat?

A. Nectar

4 How far do southward migrating butterflies travel?

A. Up to 3,000 miles (4,800 km)

5 How long is the pupa inside the chrysalis?

A. Two weeks

6 Where do monarch butterflies spend their summers?

A. In the meadows

7 In how many places to eastern monarchs gather?

A. About 12

8 When do monarchs begin the journey north?

A. In the second week of March

9 What are the best plants for a butterfly garden?

A. Milkweed and nectar plants

10 How do butterflies tell the time?

A. By using their antennae

KEY WORDS

antennae: Antennae are thin feelers on an insect's head. A monarch butterfly has antennae.

basks: A butterfly basks when it spreads its wings to take in heat from the sunshine. A monarch butterfly basks in the sun.

chrysalis: A chrysalis is a butterfly in the stage between caterpillar and adult. Inside a chrysalis is a pupa.

habitat: A habitat is a place that has the food, water, and shelter an animal needs to survive. The monarch's summer habitat has milkweed plants.

hatches: An animal hatches when it breaks out of its egg. A monarch caterpillar hatches on a milkweed plant.

host plant: A host plant is a plant that is used for food for new caterpillars. The monarch's host plant is the milkweed plant.

metamorphosis: Metamorphosis is the series of changes some animals go through between hatching and adulthood. A monarch butterfly goes through a metamorphosis from larva to adult.

molts: When a caterpillar molts, it sheds old skin and grows new skin. A monarch caterpillar molts a few times.

nectar: Nectar is a sweet liquid produced by flowers. Monarch butterflies drink nectar for food.

population: A population is all the animals of one type that live in the same area. A monarch butterfly population flies to the oyamel forests.

predators: Predators are animals that hunt and eat other animals. Colors on a monarch's body tell predators to stay away.

proboscis: A proboscis is the tongue of a butterfly that curls up. A butterfly drinks nectar with its proboscis.

pupa: A pupa is an insect in the life cycle stage between larva and adult. A monarch pupa changes in its chrysalis.

seasonal: Seasonal is something related to the seasons of the year. Monarch butterflies have a seasonal migration.

INDEX

Log on to www.av2books.com

AV² by Weigl brings you media enhanced books that support active learning. Go to www.av2books.com, and enter the special code found on page 2 of this book. You will gain access to enriched and enhanced content that supplements and complements this book. Content includes video, audio, weblinks, quizzes, a slide show, and activities.

AV² Online Navigation

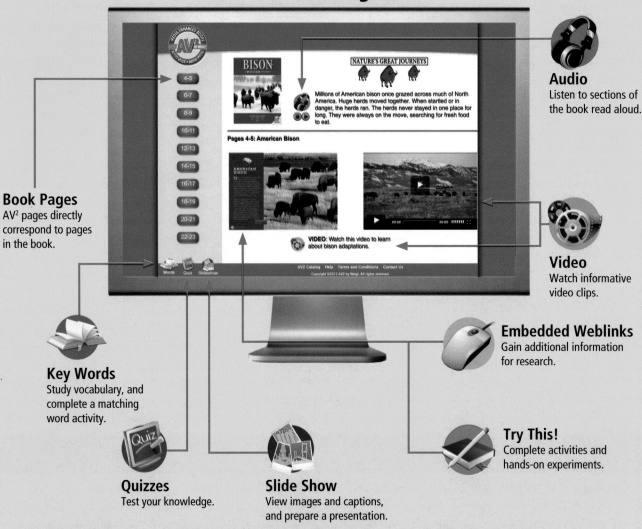

Audio
Listen to sections of the book read aloud.

Book Pages
AV² pages directly correspond to pages in the book.

Video
Watch informative video clips.

Key Words
Study vocabulary, and complete a matching word activity.

Embedded Weblinks
Gain additional information for research.

Quizzes
Test your knowledge.

Slide Show
View images and captions, and prepare a presentation.

Try This!
Complete activities and hands-on experiments.

AV² was built to bridge the gap between print and digital. We encourage you to tell us what you like and what you want to see in the future.

Sign up to be an AV² Ambassador at www.av2books.com/ambassador.

Due to the dynamic nature of the Internet, some of the URLs and activities provided as part of AV² by Weigl may have changed or ceased to exist. AV² by Weigl accepts no responsibility for any such changes. All media enhanced books are regularly monitored to update addresses and sites in a timely manner. Contact AV² by Weigl at 1-866-649-3445 or av2books@weigl.com with any questions, comments, or feedback.